KT-451-127

Ideas of the Modern World

Feminism

Kaye Stearman

049757

THE HENLEY COLLEGE LIBRARY

Copyright © Hodder Wayland 2003

Published in Great Britain in 2003 by Hodder
Wayland, a division of Hodder Children's Books.

This paperback edition published in 2005.

Series design: Simon Borrough
Proof reader: David C. Sills, Proof Positive
Reading Services

The right of Kaye Stearman to be identified as
the author of this work has been asserted by her
in accordance with the Copyright, Designs and
Patents Act 1988.

All rights reserved. Apart from any use
permitted under UK copyright law, this
publication may only be reproduced, stored or
transmitted, in any form, or by any means with
prior permission in writing of the publishers
or in the case of reprographic production in
accordance with the terms of licences issued
by the Copyright Licensing Agency.

British Library Cataloguing in Publication Data
Stearman, Kaye
Feminism. – (Ideas of the modern world)
1. Feminism – Juvenile literature
I. Title
305'4'2

ISBN 0 7502 4365 1

Printed in China by WKT

Hodder Children's Books
A division of Hodder Headline Limited
338 Euston Road, London NW1 3BH

Acknowledgements
The author extends special thanks to Frances
Connelly and Imogen Rhia Herrad for their
knowledge and encouragement.

The author and publishers thank the following
for permission to reproduce photographs:

Mary Evans Picture Library: pages 12 (bottom),
17, 19, 20, 21, 28; Mary Evans/The Women's
Library: pages 13, 16; Hodder Wayland Picture
Library: pages 6, 9, 24; Hodder Wayland Picture
Library/National Portrait Gallery, London: page
12 (top); Hodder Wayland Picture
Library/Planned Parenthood World Population,
USA: page 29; Popperfoto: pages 4, 10, 11, 25,
30, 34, 35, 43, 44, 49, 50, 51, 52, 54, 55, 58;
Popperfoto/Reuter: page 59; Rex Features:
pages 7, 46, 57; Topham/Associated Press: page
31; Topham Picturepoint: pages 14, 22, 23, 27,
33, 37, 38, 39, 41, 42, 45, 47, 48, 53, 56 (and title
page).

Cover photo shows a group of businesswomen
(Digital Vision)

Contents

What is Feminism?

Although feminist ideas have been around for centuries, the term feminism is a relatively new one, first used in 1895. Put simply, it means that women and girls should have equal **human rights** with men and boys, and equal roles and responsibilities in society. A feminist is a person, a woman or man, who supports feminism.

Feminism can refer both to ideas about women's role, **status** and history, and to actions, such as campaigns for women's rights. Feminist ideas have been developed by individuals and small groups.

Fighting for a better life: a feminist demonstration for improved pay and conditions in Guatemala in October 2002.

A feminist movement occurs when large numbers of people try to put ideas into action.

Waves of feminism

Feminism is a fairly new movement.
It began at the end of the eighteenth century, continued on and off throughout the nineteenth, and became most active in the twentieth century. Feminism is sometimes classified into 'waves': 'first-wave feminism' refers to women's campaigns for the vote between 1890 and 1920 (see pages 18 to 26); 'second-wave feminism' refers to the **Women's Liberation** movement between 1965 and 1980 (see pages 35 to 44). Some people say that today we live in the era of 'third-wave feminism', based on women's '**empowerment**'. Others say it should be called 'post-feminism' (meaning 'after feminism'), but it is far too early to name and judge our own times.

The different faces of feminism

Feminism has changed over time and continues to change. It is not one idea or movement, but many. A recent book, *A Reader's Companion to US Women's History*, lists seventeen major types of feminism in the USA alone, including American Indian, Arab American, Asian American, Jewish, Latina, Lesbian, Marxist, Puerto Rican and Working Class. Worldwide there are many more variations of feminism – and big differences between them. Some are revolutionary, seeking major changes to how society is run, others seek smaller, more gradual changes.

Although most feminists believe in equality between women and men, some say that women are superior to men – even that men are not necessary. Feminism has no leaders, uniforms, structures or parliaments. Unlike many modern movements, it does not promote or use violence and nearly all feminist activity has been peaceful and non-violent.

Whatever we think of feminism, it has already made huge changes to the way many people think, act and behave, and to the way women and men live and work. Although feminist ideas are now widely accepted in many countries, feminism itself remains highly controversial. This is because our ideas about gender and equality are deeply influenced by our upbringing, our culture, religion and way of life. And, although societies change, we often hold on to older ideas about the roles of women and men.

The playground test

Look at children at play in any primary school playground. Most boys run, jump, shove and shout. Most girls cluster in small groups, walking, skipping, playing and talking. Why does this happen? Is it just natural, or is it that even young children have learnt to behave according to **gender roles**?

Gender differences

People who disagree with feminism may argue that women and men can never be equal because their bodies and – more controversially – their minds function differently. Even as small children there are sometimes pronounced differences in attitudes and behaviour between boys and girls. As children grow into adults, the differences become more apparent.

Women scientists at work. For centuries women have been denied equal opportunities with men in education and employment.

The single biggest difference is biological – women can get pregnant and have children. But why should biological differences mean that women are treated unequally or are given fewer rights than men?

The Mosuo people in China belong to an unusual, woman-centred society.

Women and equality

A society in which men are dominant is called a patriarchal society and one in which women are dominant is called a matriarchal society. Some people believe that matriarchal societies may have been more common in the past. Against the odds, some matriarchal societies, like the Mosuo (see box and photo), still survive today.

It is difficult to find societies where women and men are treated completely equally. Women are less likely than men to own land or property, receive an education, earn their own money, or have a say in how society is run. Despite the huge changes of the past two centuries, this is still largely true today.

A woman-centred society

The Mosuo people live in a remote area of south-west China. Mosuo society is built around women. The oldest woman is the family decision-maker. Daughters do not marry and move away, but stay in their mother's household with their children. Sons also remain with their mother. The money they earn will support their sisters' children, rather than their own. The Chinese government has tried to change the Mosuo, but the Mosuo prefer the older, woman-centred ways.

Raising the Issues

Most women and men have accepted their place in society but, over the centuries, a few exceptional individuals have challenged traditional ideas. In thirteenth-century France, a noblewoman known as Christine of Pizan (c.1340–1430) wrote a long manuscript called 'The City of Ladies', which described a view of history in which women were seen to be every bit as good and righteous as men.

Such individuals were unusual. Sometimes their ideas gained a following and influenced society, but most were laughed at or ignored. However, at crucial times, new **philosophies** and ways of looking at the world really do make a difference to huge numbers of people, even though change may take place over decades or centuries.

A fair share for women

One Sura (chapter) of the Qur'an is called 'al-Nisa' (women) and contains rules for the fair treatment of women. One section says:

'Men should have a share in what their parents and kinsmen leave; and women should have a share in what their parents and kinsmen leave; whether it be little or much, they shall be legally entitled to a share.'

New rights

From the seventh century, women gained new rights under the **radical** new religion of Islam which swept rapidly across Arabia and the Middle East. Women had few rights in traditional Arab society. They lived under the **guardianship** of their fathers, brothers and husbands and were inherited, like cattle or palm trees. In a break with the past, the Prophet Muhammad (c.570–632) decreed that women had rights to divorce, to child maintenance and to inherit land and property. These rights were expressed in very precise terms, and were outlined in the holy book, the Qur'an, and Islamic laws. While women did not have equality with men, they did have real legal rights that could be enforced by religious courts.

The Enlightenment

The ideas that gave birth to feminism grew from radical and revolutionary movements in eighteenth-century Europe and, later, North America. In a movement known as 'the Enlightenment' (c.1650–1789), **philosophers** questioned traditional religious beliefs. They also challenged the absolute power held by monarchs and a society in which people's social position was based on birth rather than on merit.

The Qur'an is the holy book of Islam. It outlines, among other things, the rights and responsibilities of women and men.

The unknown feminist

In 2002, a 182-page manuscript by an unknown author was discovered in the vaults of Wigan town hall in northern England. Titled 'Woman's Worth', it argued that women were more intelligent, religious, virtuous, charitable and wise than men, and quoted the Bible in support of its arguments. Historians say that the manuscript was written between 1630 and 1640, and is the first feminist document in English:

'I say that shee [women] should have preheminency [authority] and bare rule over men, but I have no sooner spoken of power and authorite but mee thinkes I heare some man begin to interrupt mee and go about to stop my mouth with that punishment which was layd upon women.'

Rather than religion, the Enlightenment philosophers drew on 'reason' – rational and scientific ways of seeing the world. They looked at new and different ways of organizing society based upon individual merit. Rather than emphasizing a person's duties to society, they talked about people's rights in society. These rights included the freedom to think, believe and speak without **censorship** or punishment by the Church or government, and to vote for government representatives. These ideas laid the basis of our modern system of **human rights**.

Revolution

Later attempts to define and extend people's rights came in the American and French **revolutions**. In 1776, thirteen British colonies in North America declared their independence and, after winning the subsequent war, became the founders of the present United States of America. Their Declaration of Independence stated: '…that all men are created equal, that they are endowed by their creator with

The US Declaration of Independence in 1776 was a landmark in human rights. Nevertheless, from the picture below, no women appear to have been present at its signing.

Women revolutionaries march to Versailles, the seat of the French monarchy. But despite the important role played by women in the French revolution, none were included in the Declaration of the Rights of Man.

certain inalienable rights, that among these are life, liberty and the pursuit of happiness.' Thirteen years later, when the people of France rose up against its corrupt, **despotic** monarchy, the new revolutionary government used similar words in its Declaration of the Rights of Man.

However, in both America and France, these rights did not extend to women or to other groups such as slaves, native peoples or gypsies. These people had few rights and were discriminated against in law, economically and socially. It may seem strange that men who proclaimed themselves revolutionaries, determined to overturn the old order and promote human rights, could completely ignore women's rights, but ideas about women were deeply held and rarely questioned. Many revolutionaries saw women as inferior, weak in mind and body and needing protection, an image that hid the fact that most women lived harsh lives. Others felt that men could exercise rights on behalf of women.

11

Mary Wollstonecraft was a pioneering feminist thinker, writer and activist.

'Hyenas in petticoats'

However, two remarkable women did speak out. Mary Wollstonecraft (1759-97) was an independent Englishwoman who lived in revolutionary France and earned her living as a writer. Her book, *A **Vindication** of the Rights of Women*, argued that the new rights should also belong to women. A French woman, Olympe de Gouges, rewrote the Declaration of the Rights of Man to include women. Both authors argued that women needed extra rights, such as a right to equality in education, and in marriage, where a husband had legal and financial power over his wife. Critics viciously attacked both authors. Mary Wollstonecraft was branded a 'hyena in petticoats'. Olympe de Gouges was executed in part because of her support for women's rights. Their brave words and remarkable lives were forgotten during the course of the following century.

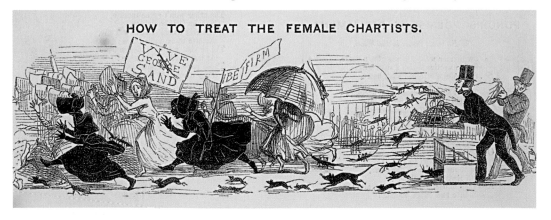

HOW TO TREAT THE FEMALE CHARTISTS.

Women were active in the British Chartist movement for greater rights but, as the cartoon above shows, they were often ridiculed by men.

Voting reforms

In the nineteenth century, a series of revolutionary political movements swept across Europe. They demanded more democratic government structures, including the vote for all men, regardless of wealth or **status**. Sometimes women were included in these demands, but mostly they were not. For example, in

Britain the **Chartist** movement, active from 1838 to 1848, called for all men to have the right to vote, but did not go so far as to seek votes for women. The **liberal** philosopher, John Stuart Mill argued strongly that women should be granted the same civil and political rights as men. In 1867 when he was an MP (Member of Parliament) he proposed a bill which gave the vote to women, but it was heavily defeated in the House of Commons.

Elizabeth Garrett Anderson, one of the first women doctors, and Emily Davies present a petition on women's rights to John Stuart Mill MP in 1860.

Olympe de Gouges (1746-93)

Olympe de Gouges (born Maire Gouze) was a writer and political **activist**. She was an enthusiastic supporter of the French Revolution of 1789 but protested at the exclusion of women from the Declaration of the Rights of Man. In 1791 she rewrote the document as the Declaration of the Rights of Woman, proclaiming that: 'women were superior to men in beauty and courage in maternal suffering' and should have rights to 'life, liberty, property and, especially, resistance to oppression'. However, the new government soon turned against women activists. In November 1793, Olympe de Gouges was accused of treason and executed by the guillotine.

In nineteenth-century Britain, poor women existed in conditions of deprivation and hardship, and feminist ideas were not always relevant to their lives.

Unjust laws

A few women and men sought to change particular unjust laws. For example in England, where women were considered to be legal minors (children) rather than responsible adults, the writer Caroline Norton campaigned for the right of a divorced woman to keep her own property and earnings, and for custody of her children. She declared in court: 'I have no rights, only wrongs.' Many women, including Queen Victoria, the British monarch, believed that it was natural for women and men to occupy separate, unequal roles in society. In 1868, Victoria wrote: '[We] must join in checking this mad, wicked folly of 'Women's Rights' with all its attendant horrors.'

The anti-slavery movement

It was not surprising that the call for women's rights was stronger in less traditional societies such as North America. Here social injustice, such as the oppression of people as slaves, was meeting with widespread opposition. However, while northern US states gradually abolished slavery most southern states regarded slave labour as vital to their economies. Anti-slavery campaigners, known as abolitionists, argued that all slaves should be granted their freedom with equal rights. Some campaigners helped slaves to escape to Canada or to northern states. As with earlier radical movements, some women, and a few men, saw a parallel between slavery and their own lack of rights. But most male abolitionists regarded women who spoke out against slavery as 'unwomanly' and even tried to stop them from speaking. Angelina Grimke (1805-79), a leading activist, wrote: 'We are placed very unexpectedly in the forefront of an entirely new contest – a contest for the rights of woman as a moral, intelligent and responsible being.'

It was not until slavery was abolished in 1865 that women's rights could come to the fore. Despite the fact that all men, including former slaves, were regarded as citizens and had the right to vote for representatives to national and state governments, women were not allowed to vote or take part in public life. Demands for equality were first formally put forward at the first women's rights **convention** at Seneca Falls in 1848.

The Seneca Falls Convention

Seneca Falls in upper New York State became an important meeting place for the anti-slavery and women's rights movements. America's first women's rights convention in 1848 was organized by Elizabeth Cady Stanton and Lucretia Mott. They drew up a Declaration of Sentiments, a new version of the Declaration of Independence, demanding property rights for women, equal pay for equal work and the right to vote. Three hundred people attended the convention. Of the 68 women who signed the Seneca Falls declaration, only one, Charlotte Woodward, lived to see American women win the vote in 1920.

For the next half century, the women's rights movement in the USA was dominated by a remarkable partnership of two women – Susan B. Anthony (1820-1906) and Elizabeth Cady Stanton (1815-1902). Together they organized meetings and wrote books and pamphlets on many issues – social movements such as temperance (anti-alcohol), and legal reforms such as the right for women to inherit and keep property. Above all, they pressed for a greater **democracy**, giving all women the right to vote and to stand for election to government bodies. They formed the National Women's **Suffrage** Association in 1869.

American feminist leader, Susan B. Anthony.

Women and the vote

In 1872 Anthony attempted and failed to vote in the presidential election. The two women realized that changes were needed to the US **constitution**. From 1878, each year sympathetic congressmen put forward an **amendment** extending voting rights to women. Each year the amendment was ignored or rejected by the all-male Congress. There was some success at state level. In 1869, Wyoming became the first US territory to grant votes to women and, slowly, other states followed its example.

Neither Anthony nor Stanton lived to see US women receive the full rights of citizens in 1920. In Europe, despite individual victories, progress was even slower. In both continents the battle over ideas about women's rights only touched the lives of a relatively small

'We little dreamed... '

At the end of her life, Susan B. Anthony looked back on her work with both disappointment and pride:

'We little dreamed when we began this contest that half a century later we would be compelled to leave the finish of the battle to another generation of women. But our hearts are filled with joy to know that they enter this task equipped with a college education, with business experience, with the freely admitted right to speak in public – all of which were denied to women fifty years ago.'

number of educated middle-class women, who were frustrated by their inferior legal status and limited opportunities. Most working-class women in the slums and factories of the growing industrial towns and cities led lives of hardship and deprivation, and legal rights or access to higher education had little direct relevance to their lives. However, by the end of the nineteenth century, a radical mass feminist movement had begun to emerge.

Many feminists organized protests against alcohol, which they said destroyed homes and families. This scene of women demonstrating outside a bar comes from Logan, Ohio, USA in 1874.

Elizabeth Blackwell (1821-1910)

Against male opposition, Elizabeth Blackwell became the first woman doctor of modern times. She applied to twenty-eight medical schools before being accepted at Geneva College in New York where she graduated as head of her class. She then studied at La Maternité hospital in Paris and St Bartholomew's hospital in London, where she made a lifelong friend in Florence Nightingale, the founder of modern nursing. She returned to New York where she established a clinic and hospital for women and, in 1868, the first Women's Medical College. Her younger sister, Emily Blackwell (1826-1910), became the first woman surgeon. Throughout her long life Elizabeth Blackwell campaigned for better public health and for women to have the opportunity to pursue careers in medicine.

Campaigning for the Vote

A new century is often a time of new ideas and standards. In the 1890s many women in Europe and the USA questioned their inferior place in society. Often these were younger, better educated women who described themselves as 'new women', seeking freedom from marriage and domestic duties. Rather than remain at home, supported by fathers and husbands, single middle-class women entered the growing office workforce as typists and clerks. Their new lives were reflected in their clothing and leisure activities. In 1895, the term 'feminist' was coined to describe people who supported women's rights.

Social reform

Social reformers launched campaigns to improve women's lives – for better education and employment opportunities, to reform marriage, divorce and property laws, and for social equality. Women were active supporters of the temperance movement, which campaigned against alcohol, regarded as a major social evil against women and children. They painted a vivid picture of how working men spent all their wages on drink, resulting in hungry families, domestic violence and broken homes.

For poor women the situation was stark – low wages, insecurity, bad housing, domestic violence, racism. In many countries, women workers joined the **trade union** movement, despite opposition by employers. There were notable successes – for example, young women at a match factory in London's East End won their strike in 1888 – but most women remained without union protection. Some feminists worked with the new **socialist parties** who were sending

The match girls of London's East End, who successfully won their strike for better conditions in 1888.

their first representatives to parliaments. Women who were even more **radical** joined revolutionary movements that aimed to overthrow **despotic** governments in Russia and Eastern Europe.

Universal suffrage

However, one issue came to dominate feminist activity in the years before the First World War. This was women's **suffrage** – the right to vote and be elected to government on the same terms as men. By the beginning of the twentieth century, adult men had voting rights in most Western countries. The only countries in which women could vote were New Zealand, which gave women suffrage in 1893, and Australia, which followed in 1902. In 1905 Finland became the first European country to grant the vote to women. All these countries were **democracies**, with strong trade unions and women's suffrage was accepted relatively easily. The same was not true in countries with larger populations, where the division between rich and poor was greater. Here, the ruling authorities successfully opposed granting women the vote – sometimes for decades.

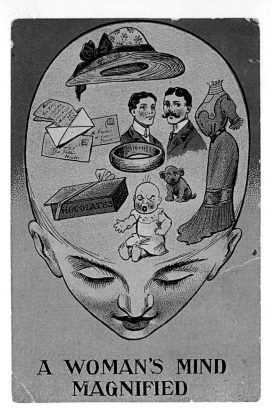

A WOMAN'S MIND MAGNIFIED

An anti-feminist cartoon shows women as empty-headed creatures interested only in marriage, clothes and babies.

A better world?

For feminists, the vote was much more important than the act of marking a paper and placing it in a ballot box. It was a symbol of a much wider issue about women's rights and participation in society. Feminists believed that women's concerns would always be neglected when governments were elected only by men. Only by using their voting power could women make government better, fairer, more caring and less selfish because, they argued, women themselves had these qualities.

Early feminists argued that, as mothers and homemakers, women had more interest in peace than war, more concern for the weak than the powerful. They said that their purity of mind and body would enable them to rise above the selfish and corrupt men in positions of power. Some **anti-feminists** used similar arguments to draw opposing conclusions, stating that women were too good and high-minded to sully themselves with political matters, which should be left to men. The most extreme opponents argued that granting women the vote would be dangerous: that it would destroy female purity, undermine male authority, create discord within families and, ultimately, lead to the breakdown of ordered society.

The most famous suffrage campaign was fought in Britain. Initially the campaign, led by the National Union of Women's Suffrage Societies (the British version of the US National

An army of women

Emmeline Pankhurst believed that women would only win the vote by acting as a united, **militant** force. In 1912 she addressed a mass meeting thus:

'Tonight I feel more than ever that we are reviewing our forces. In an army you need unity of purpose. In an army you also need unity of policy.'

Women's Suffrage Association), was low-key and peaceful. However, in 1903, Emmeline and Christabel Pankhurst led a breakaway group and formed the Women's Social and Political Union (WSPU). This group used militant **direct action** campaigns (see box) to focus attention on its cause. Between 1905 and 1914, more than 1,000 women were arrested and imprisoned. Some went on hunger strike and were force-fed by prison officials, to widespread revulsion.

LA VIE ILLUSTRÉE

LES FEMMES RÉCLAMENT LE DROIT DE VOTE

Direct action

The WSPU developed eye-catching and imaginative direct action campaigns to gain public attention for their cause. At various times they interrupted election meetings, broke shop windows, blew-up post boxes and chained themselves to the Ladies' Gallery at the Houses of Parliament. Not all feminists supported such tactics – some thought they were undignified stunts that did little to help poorer women. They pointed out that it was only richer women – who didn't have to work for their living and had servants to look after their families – who could afford to get arrested and spend time in jail. Instead these feminists gave practical support to poorer women through, for example, **law reform**, and campaigning for **social security** and maternity benefits. Nevertheless, many thousands of women joined in peaceful demonstrations in support of the WSPU.

A French language magazine of 1906 highlights the actions of militant suffragettes in Britain.

High profile tactics

The American movement was longer established than that in the UK, thanks to the pioneering work of the National Women's Suffrage Association (see page 16). This continued to press for an **amendment** to the US **constitution**, but without success. There was more success at state level and, by 1915, fifteen out of forty-eight states had women's suffrage. However, younger women were more impatient and, inspired by British feminists, they developed high profile tactics. Rather than getting involved in mass arrests, they addressed public meetings and used the new media of radio, telephone and public

The Pankhurst family

Emmeline Pankhurst (1858-1928) founded the Women's Franchise League in 1889, after seeing women's oppression at first-hand through her social work in Manchester. In 1903, with her eldest daughter, Christabel (1880-1958), she founded the women-only Women's Social and Political Union (WSPU) with one aim: 'Votes for women'. Together they developed the WSPU's militant, high profile tactics. Both were arrested and jailed many times; once Christabel fled to France to avoid arrest. Both women were brilliant, inspiring speakers; one WSPU rally drew an audience of half a million. Another daughter, Sylvia (1882-1960) was also a **suffragette**, but broke with the WSPU in 1912 to concentrate on work with the working-class women of London's East End. Another daughter, Adela Pankhurst (1885-1961) organized women in trade unions in Australia. In 1914, Emmeline and Christabel supported the government war effort while Sylvia became an anti-war **activist**.

Emmeline and Christabel Pankhurst pose in their prison clothes – both were arrested and imprisoned many times.

advertising. Some forged links with the **labour movement** and with immigrant and black women in the big cities who were fighting for racial equality. Yet, by the time war broke out in Europe in 1914, women's suffrage appeared to be as distant as ever.

Women in white: Danish suffragists celebrate gaining the vote in 1915.

The First World War

The war had a profound and unforeseen effect on feminists and feminism. In the years before 1914, feminism had begun to cross international borders and language barriers. While there had always been strong links between Britain and America, campaigners now travelled widely and feminist ideas were translated into many languages. Some feminists were also socialists and **pacifists** and were especially interested in building international links. The First World War forced feminists to choose between patriotism – loyalty to their country – and their international links. Like the general population, most chose patriotism. Even the militant WSPU immediately abandoned its campaign and threw its energies into the war effort. However, some feminists opposed the war. One thousand women peace campaigners from twelve countries met in the Netherlands (which was neutral during the war) in April 1915. They called on all governments to stop the slaughter and to give women the vote.

During the First World War women stepped into men's jobs, undertaking work that was considered difficult, dangerous and unfeminine.

War work

The four-year war affected the lives of European women in many ways. As young men went off to fight, women stepped into the jobs they had left behind. On the production lines, in public transport and in the public services, women worked long hours, often in dangerous conditions. Others served as nurses, at home and abroad. For years, women had been told that many such jobs were degrading and unfeminine, but now war work had become a matter of patriotic duty. Nevertheless, women were paid much lower rates than men and most still had to cook, clean and care for children too.

The war made the issue of women's suffrage less controversial. Seeing women taking on new roles and responsibilities broke down some of the prejudices about women's abilities and place in society and led to a more reasoned approach by governments. The neutral nations of Norway and Denmark granted women the vote in 1913 and 1915 respectively.

Amid the upheaval of **revolution**, Russian women got the vote in 1918, followed by the new nations of Austria, Czechoslovakia and Poland. Some governments used the vote to reward women for their war efforts. Canada gave the vote to army nurses in 1917 and extended it to all women later in 1918. British women over the age of thirty got the vote in 1918. But younger women had to wait until 1928 before they could vote equally with men, at the age of twenty-one. American women were awarded voting rights in 1920.

Women for peace

Carrie Chapman Catt (1859-1947) was president of the National American Women's Suffrage Association from 1915. In 1918, as peace was being declared, she demanded a place for women at the negotiating table:

'In every treaty at the close of previous wars, the seeds of new wars have lain dormant. If women are not heard at the peace conference now to be held, this war will not have been a war to end wars.'

Her first vote – a woman takes her family to the polls in Britain, 1918.

Did gaining of the vote change society and make women's lives better? The war brought huge political and economic upheavals. There were violent revolutions in Russia and China and uprisings in several European countries. Where parliamentary government survived, socialist and left-wing parties were represented in greater numbers. But, in themselves, the new votes from women had little effect on political life. Women, like men, voted according to their political beliefs or the class to which they belonged.

The way forward
Suffragists had proclaimed that, when women entered politics, public life would become more caring and less selfish. A few politicians did become more sensitive to women's concerns, introducing laws to promote girls' education and greater equality in public life. In some countries, including Denmark, women-only parties stood at elections, but their success was limited. Generally, few women stood for political office and even fewer were elected. With the vote won, feminists considered how they should go forward into the future.

Better late than not at all

For women in many countries, the gaining of voting rights was a slow process. France only granted women's suffrage in 1944 and Switzerland in 1971. In a few countries, women still do not have the right to vote or stand for elections on the same basis as men.

The Forgotten Years of Feminism

Between the First World War and the late 1960s, feminist ideas were less visible than before. As arguments for women's **suffrage** became widely accepted, it seemed that feminism had won its major battle. Most remaining feminist organizations focused on specific issues such as **law reform**, working conditions, **contraception** and **abortion**.

On the surface there had been huge changes. The 1920s brought greater personal freedom for many women in Europe and the United States. Women abandoned elaborate heavy clothing for shorter skirts, lighter materials and casual styles. Many had their long hair cut into short bobs, went to nightclubs, danced to jazz music, smoked cigarettes and drank alcohol – all symbols of the new freedom. More women entered higher education and earned and spent their own money, especially on the new consumer goods. But women still faced barriers to equality. Men were seen as the main breadwinners and were always paid more than women. In many European countries, married women were often barred from professional jobs, such as teaching, medicine and the civil service.

The 1920s saw many women gain greater personal freedoms, reflected in their looser clothing and shorter hair.

Birth control

Some feminists began to promote information about sexuality and contraception, so that women could better understand how their bodies worked and decide for themselves how many children they wanted. This was highly controversial, especially at a time when most sexual information was subject to **censorship**, unmarried mothers were regarded as shameful and methods of contraception were limited. Governments and religious organizations often opposed birth control. Pioneers, such as Margaret Sanger in the USA and Marie Stopes (1880–1958) in Britain, published information on contraception and set up clinics for poor women. Birth rates fell in many Western countries as women married later and found ways to limit births.

Socialism and communism

Some feminists argued that feminist aims could only be achieved as part of a wider political movement, such as **socialism** or **communism**, which aimed to bring sweeping revolutionary changes to society. Women joined political uprisings in

The same rights

The Russian Constitution of 1936, Article 122 states that:

'In Soviet Russia a woman enjoys the same rights as a man in all aspects of economic, cultural, public and political life.'

One of Britain's first birth control clinics, founded by Marie Stopes.

Margaret Sanger, a feminist and supporter of birth control, talks to women in New York.

Russia, Germany and China, although only in Russia did the **revolution** succeed when the Bolsheviks (the Communist Party) seized power in 1917 and established the new Soviet Union. The Russian revolution was the result of defeat on the military front, and corruption, hardship and starvation at home. Many women welcomed the revolution, hoping it would bring them a better and freer life.

Before the war, many Russian feminists had embraced revolutionary and socialist ideas, arguing that women could only achieve equality by destroying the power of the monarchy and Church. Most women lived in poverty, domestic violence was widespread and only 20 per cent could read and write.

Margaret Sanger (1879-1965)

Margaret Sanger witnessed the suffering of poor women while working as a nurse and midwife in New York. In 1916 she opened a clinic to help women escape unwanted pregnancies and to give information on birth control methods. She was arrested and jailed but later won her case and went on to found more than three hundred clinics. In 1952 she became the first president of the International Planned Parenthood Federation and supported the development of **oral contraceptive** pills.

The new Soviet government included leading feminists, such as Alexandra Kollontai. It passed laws that gave women new rights: to vote, to civil marriage (which had previously been controlled by the Church), to divorce, to receive equal pay and maternity leave. With so many men killed in the war, women were encouraged to work in industry, and the government established nurseries and communal kitchens to provide cheap and nourishing meals. Educational campaigns were targeted at women and, in a few years, there was a dramatic increase in the number of women who could read and write.

Soviet women farmworkers in the 1920s. Women were expected to do the same heavy work as men.

Dictatorship

Whatever the laws said on paper, the reality was rather different. Although conditions became more stable during the 1920s, the country was still poor and backward. Equal pay laws were not enforced and the best-paid jobs went to men. There were never enough nurseries, and the communal kitchens soon closed. At home, women still carried the burden of cooking, shopping and housework. Political control remained with a small number of men. After 1930, when the dictator Joseph Stalin took complete control of the Soviet Union, women began to lose some of the rights they had gained earlier and feminists who criticized the government were imprisoned or exiled. It seemed that it was fine for women to feature on revolutionary posters, but not to express revolutionary feminist ideas.

The Soviet Union was a country where information was tightly controlled, and it had little contact with the outside world. Nevertheless, some foreigners did visit and brought home glowing reports of how well women were doing and how communism had helped feminism. Some Western feminists joined communist, socialist or other left-wing parties, arguing that the limited feminist reforms that had occurred in some countries would only be of benefit to better-off women. They argued that real equality for poor women would come only after political revolution. In 1929, a severe and widespread economic slump, known as the Great Depression, brought about huge unemployment and mounting poverty in Western countries. It seemed to confirm that, by itself, feminism could not overcome poverty or inequality for women.

Alexandra Kollontai, a feminist revolutionary, fought for women's rights in the Soviet Union.

Alexandra Kollontai (1872-1952)

Born of a Russian noble family, Alexandra Kollontai became a writer and revolutionary in Switzerland. She urged that women should have equality with men in all matters, including **sexual equality**. In 1914 she joined the Bolshevik Party and after the 1917 revolution became the commissioner for social welfare, pushing through new laws to assist women. She lost influence under the rule of Stalin (1930-53) and left the government. She went on to serve as Soviet ambassador to Norway, Mexico and Sweden – the first woman ambassador of modern times.

Fascism

As unemployment brought poverty and misery to many, a political movement – **fascism** – began to take root in Italy, Germany and Japan. In Germany, the post-war **constitution** had given women equal rights with men. However, women's gains in work, welfare and politics were reversed following the election in 1933 of the National Socialist Party (Nazis) to government. The Nazis believed in the supremacy of their people – an imagined 'Aryan' race of 'pure', fair-haired, blue-eyed Germans – who would eventually rule the world. While German men fought battles, the Nazis thought that the role of German women was to support them, as childbearers and homemakers. German schools taught domestic education to prepare girls for motherhood. Feminist books were confiscated and burned. The Nazis saw feminists as dangerous and **subversive** opponents and banned, imprisoned and exiled them.

Not surprisingly, most feminists opposed fascism and gave their support to anti-fascist movements. As the world slipped towards another global war, many feminists supported **pacifist** movements, arguing that war could never benefit society and would place extra burdens on women. Having seen one dreadful war, they felt it was a feminist duty to prevent another.

Her most glorious duty

Joseph Goebbels, German minister for propaganda, 1933-45, stated that:

'A woman's most fitting place is in the family, and the most glorious duty she can fulfil is to present her people and her country with a child.'

The Second World War

The outbreak of the Second World War in 1939 saw governments re-evaluate women's roles. As in the first war, women were needed to fill men's jobs – including those that had previously been 'unsuitable for women'. Women worked on the land, in heavy industries and in essential services, such as transport. Many joined the military forces overseas, although not in combat roles. While most women volunteered, whether out of patriotism or necessity, some governments made it compulsory for women to work. For example, in the countries occupied by the Nazis and their allies, women and men were forced into slave labour. Women everywhere were in the front-line as civilians. Their homes were occupied and destroyed, and they were compelled to forage for food amid the destruction.

As the Second World War ended, women were expected to give up their jobs and salaries to the returning men. Many women were sacked or given 'women's jobs' such as secretaries or cleaners at lower pay. But, as with the First World War, there could be no return to the past. In the **allied countries**, women were stronger and more confident; their efforts had helped to win the war and resist oppression and they expected a better life as a reward. In France, women were finally given the vote in 1944. Democratic governments were introduced in the defeated countries of Germany, Italy and Japan, with laws giving equal rights to women.

The home front: women workers in a steel factory, taking men's places during the Second World War.

The ideal home and family — as widely portrayed in the 1950s.

Simone de Beauvoir (1908-86)

Simone de Beauvoir was a brilliant student who went on to become one of France's leading **philosophers**. With her lifelong partner, Jean-Paul Sartre and other philosophers she developed a **philosophy** known as Existentialism, which rejected traditional religious and social rules and emphasized individual choice. *The Second Sex*, de Beauvoir's most famous book, explored women's lives through an examination of history, literature and philosophy. She argued that women are seen as 'the other' and forced by education and tradition to occupy an inferior place in society. Instead women should aim to be truly free human beings.

In the 1950s, Western countries recovered from the destruction of war, economies became more stable and prosperous. Femininity and domestic virtues were promoted, birth rates rose and many countries experienced a baby boom. Outwardly most women appeared happy with their separate roles, and feminists appeared to have no place. Yet it was at this time that one of the most influential feminist books appeared. *The Second Sex*, by Simone de Beauvoir, was published in France in 1949 and translated into English in 1953. Although it is a difficult and complex work, it became a landmark book in feminist thought and a bridge to the forthcoming era of **Women's Liberation**.

Feminism Becomes Women's Liberation

In 1960, feminism seemed to belong to the past. In 1970, feminism was the subject of passionate debate and action. This period was later referred to as 'second-wave feminism' – the first wave having been the fight for the vote. But the term 'feminism' was rarely used in 1970. Instead there was a new name – '**Women's Liberation**', often shortened to Women's Lib.

The 1960s spawned a host of new causes. In Africa and Asia many countries were struggling to gain independence from their European rulers. In the USA, the **civil rights movement** used non-violent campaigns to draw attention to the discrimination and poverty that blighted the lives of African Americans. Some campaigners went further, and supported the use of violent methods to achieve 'black liberation'. Many people protested against the USA's involvement in the Vietnam War (1964-75).

Women were active in many radical movements, including protests against American military involvement in the Vietnam War.

Hippies

Some people, 'hippies', rejected mainstream society ('dropped out') in favour of simpler, less materialistic lifestyles. While few people did so for very long, many aspects of the hippie lifestyle, whether music, sex, drugs or dress, became regular parts of people's lives. While these movements started in North America, they spread rapidly to Western Europe and Australia, aided by the power of television.

From the beginning, women had joined these movements for change, taking part in civil rights marches, protesting against the war in Vietnam and following the hippie way of life. Many assumed that they would enter these struggles on an equal footing with men. But they discovered that women in **radical** groups faced the same inequalities and lack of respect as they did in the wider world. It was taken for granted that men would do the thinking, speaking and writing, and women would do the listening, cooking and cleaning up as well as serving as sexual partners. Many women became disillusioned and asked why they should have to face discrimination in movements that proclaimed equality and justice for all.

Hippies claimed to have rejected mainstream society in favour of a better, more balanced lifestyle.

Hostility from men

Naomi Weisstein was a founding member of one of the first women's discussion groups, the Chicago Westside Group. Years later, she said of their first meetings:

'The women started to talk and we found that we couldn't stop talking. We talked about the contempt and hostility we felt from men. We were afraid to call ourselves feminists. We finally came up with "women's liberation".'

Women's freedom

Many Women's Liberation groups made declarations of their aims and values. In February 1969, Chicago Women's Liberation stated:

'What does women's freedom mean? It means freedom of self-determination, self-enrichment, the freedom to live one's own life, set one's own goals, the freedom to rejoice in one's own accomplishments.'

A Women's Liberation march in New York, USA, in 1970.

The liberation movement

Just as black people and anti–war demonstrators had formed their own movements for change, so did women. No one person or event began the Women's Liberation movement, but from the mid–1960s women began to form small groups to discuss common problems, write manifestos and plan actions. Within a few years, there were women's groups in many countries and the term Women's Liberation had become an international rallying cry.

Like the **suffragists** and many groups who try to achieve change, the Women's Liberation movement had a radical minority and a more moderate majority. The radicals said that women would achieve their liberation only through **revolution**, although there was a lot of discussion about what form this would take.

For some groups, this meant a violent political overthrow of the **capitalist system**. These radical feminists tried to build links with **trade unions** and left-wing political parties. In 1968, riots and political uprisings occurred in Europe and North America, but these proved shortlived and the political system survived. Other women rejected both **communist** and capitalist systems. They saw male power – patriarchy – as the problem, and tried to forge a society based on women's own needs, even if this meant excluding men and boys completely. This group, sometimes referred to as separatists, focused on issues such as **pornography**, rape, domestic violence and discrimination against **lesbians**.

National Organization of Women
However, most supporters of Women's Liberation did not belong to either group – they demanded far-reaching changes within the existing political and economic system. Organizations such as the National Organization of Women (NOW) in the USA or the Women's Electoral Lobby (WEL) in Australia pressed governments to change unequal laws or extend opportunities for women. These groups tended to be white and middle class, but they could summon the support of thousands of women. Many governments responded by introducing new laws and policies in support of women's rights.

In 1968 there were challenges against governments in Europe and America. This photo shows cars being used to barricade a street in Paris, France.

Betty Friedan (1921-)

Betty Friedan studied psychology at university and later worked as a journalist. Her attempts to combine marriage and family with a career were unusual in the 1950s. Friedan found many women were unhappy with their role as wives and mothers. She explored ideas about why women were so dissatisfied with their lives in her book, *The Feminine Mystique*, published in 1963. Friedan was a founder of the National Organization of Women (NOW) and served as its president until 1970.

Women's Liberation was never a unified movement. Many black women felt that it focused mainly on the problems of middle-class white women. It had little relevance to the lives of poor black women, which were dominated by daily battles with racism, poor housing, bad schools and a complex welfare system. One writer pointed out that, in 1967, black women in the USA earned only 40 per cent of the average male wage – white women earned 60 per cent. Black women began to form their own feminist movements, which author Alice Walker later described as 'womanist' ('black feminism').

Betty Friedan is one of today's best known feminist writers and activists.

Wanting more

In her bestselling book, *The Feminine Mystique*, Betty Friedan wrote:

'We can no longer ignore the voice within women that says: "I want something more than my husband, my children and my home." Who knows what women can be when they are free to become themselves?'

Consciousness-raising

In many respects, the ideas expressed by Women's Liberation went further than the earlier feminists. Liberation came not from the outside, Women's Lib argued, it had to begin with women themselves. Women had to discover who they were and what they wanted. Women began to meet in small, 'consciousness-raising' groups, talking about their lives, why they felt frustrated and angry and what they wanted to do about it. In turn, these group discussions gave rise to 'women-only' spaces such as meeting places, bookshops and cafés where women could feel safe and comfortable.

A woman's right to choose

Women's Liberation focused on personal experiences such as sex, pregnancy and childbirth. Many women still felt that they had little control over their own bodies and lives. In many countries it was difficult to obtain contraceptives or a legal **abortion**. Unwanted pregnancies were still common and desperate women sought abortions illegally. These abortions were often unsafe and unhygienic and many women died or were left with permanent injuries. It is not surprising that safe and legal abortion on request became one of the main causes of Women's Liberation. The slogan 'a woman's right to choose' summed up women's demands for control over their own bodies – without interference from government, employers, churches, family or partner.

The personal is political

The phrase 'the personal is political' shows how Women's Liberation embraced issues growing from women's personal experiences and relationships. Marriage was seen as an unequal relationship with women subordinate to men. Even when relations looked equal on the surface, underneath they were deeply unequal, especially at home where women still did the cooking, cleaning, washing and childcare. These were not just personal, isolated issues but larger problems for society as a whole. Although individual men could take responsibility for housework, women would never be free unless society saw housework as something to be valued and shared equally between women and men.

Women's Liberation also looked to the world of paid work. Women rarely had jobs of equal **status** or equal pay with men. One problem was that most jobs were categorized as male or female. Male jobs were considered to be more skilled and therefore more highly rewarded. Women's jobs were seen as less skilled and less valuable. Equal pay for equal work was a major demand. But attitudes were slow to change. While men were regarded as breadwinners, women's wages were seen as 'extras'. But as women began to marry later and divorce rates rose, more of them depended on their earnings to live. Women's Liberation supported women who went on strike, both with practical and moral support.

A longstanding aim of American feminists has been to add an Equal Rights Amendment to the US constitution. This aim has still to be achieved.

41

The contraceptive pill

In the 1960s many countries saw a greater openness about sexual matters, and scientific developments resulted in safer, more reliable **contraception**. In 1960 the **oral contraceptive** pill was introduced. By 1966 six million American women were using the pill, as were millions of other women in other countries. Despite opposition from the Roman Catholic Church and some governments, more and more women, married and unmarried, used modern birth control. For millions of women, freedom from unwanted pregnancies and the ability to decide how and when to have children was the most important right of all.

Gloria Steinem has been an active feminist since the days of Women's Liberation. This photo dates from the 1970s.

While earlier feminists had sought equality with men, Women's Liberation questioned whether equality was either possible or desirable. Why should women seek to copy men if they had produced such an unequal, unjust world? Why should women conform to standards of beauty judged by men, although these had little to do with the lives of real women? Furthermore, when society was so deeply biased against women why should women fight an unwinnable battle? The new term 'sexist' was applied to all aspects of life that discriminated against women. These and other ideas, often complex and abstract, were supported by books and articles by feminists such as Germaine Greer, Kate Millet, Gloria Steinem, Sheila Rowbotham and many others.

Women's Liberation was a very active and exciting movement. It drew huge support but also huge opposition from men and women who saw it as undermining the natural order and feminine values. Although millions of women marched and demonstrated for change, Women's Liberation was largely a movement of individual women without leaders. There were few causes that united all women – rich and poor, black and white, married and single, heterosexual and lesbian. By the 1980s, the movement had split into many factions and lost much of its vitality.

Barbara Castle was a cabinet minister in the British Labour government in the 1960s and 1970s. She introduced an Equal Pay Act in 1970.

Equal pay for equal work

Equal pay for women workers became a major cause for Women's Liberation in Britain, especially as male-dominated trade unions were not always supportive. In 1968 women machinists at the Ford Motor factory in east London went on strike for equal pay for work of equal value. Despite male hostility, they brought the factory to a standstill and won their case. In 1970, Barbara Castle, a Labour cabinet minister in the British government, introduced an Equal Pay Act, which helped to bring about greater equality. However, thirty years later women in the UK still earn less than men – even when they do the same sort of work.

Nevertheless, Women's Liberation played a vital role in feminist history. Although it was often chaotic and unrealistic, it also had many practical achievements. It brought feminist ideas to millions of women, and fought to make sure that women's experiences – not just men's – were included in the history books. It placed pressure on governments to change unequal laws and practices. Feminist ideas which had started in Western countries were adapted to women in different cultures and situations. Women's rights movements developed in Asia, Latin America, Africa and the Middle East. And feminism, in whatever form, became a normal part of many women's lives.

Women in Algeria in 2002 carry the feminist message into their own society.

Women's day off

On 24 October 1975, **United Nations** Day, women in Iceland held a 'women's day off'. The country came to a standstill as women stayed away from work or school and held meetings and demonstrations. Within a year, Iceland's Parliament had passed equal rights laws, ensuring that women were treated equally in all areas of life. By 1980, Iceland had elected a woman president, Vigdis Finnbogafdottir (1930-), who served until 1996. In Parliament, one quarter of the elected representatives are women – one of the highest proportions in the world.

I'm Not a Feminist, But...

The effects of Women's Liberation lasted much longer than the movement itself. The term 'Women's Liberation' was used less and less and the movement was often referred to as 'second-wave feminism'. Feminist ideas became widely known and debated, even if the level of understanding was sometimes low. Ideas that had once been considered outrageous began to enter mainstream thinking. Slowly, governments began responding to women's demands, enacting new laws and policies. In 1974 the new socialist government in France established a ministry of women's rights.

Some women ran for office on feminist issues but most worked through established parties. More women were elected to parliaments, although numbers were still fairly low. In the 1970s, Norway's political parties agreed to reserve places for women candidates. In eight years, the number of women representatives rose from 10 per cent to 24 per cent. By 1995, the figure was 40 per cent and the prime minister and eight cabinet members were women. But this was unusual. Where women became political leaders it was usually because they had family connections or that they were exceptional women succeeding in a man's world. Margaret Thatcher, British Conservative prime minister from 1979 to 1990, always stressed that she was not a feminist, had no interest in feminism and took no political measures to help women.

Gro Harlem Bruntland served as prime minister of Norway and then as director of the United Nations' World Health Organization.

A demonstration in London, UK, 'blows the whistle' on violence against women.

Feminists often met with resistance. In 1972 the US Congress took the first steps towards passing an Equal Rights **Amendment** to the **constitution**. However, it could only become law if it was ratified (agreed) by all US states within ten years. With fourteen states refusing to ratify, the amendment lapsed. The USA still has no constitutional guarantee of equal treatment for both sexes.

In Italy, the Roman Catholic Church campaigned to overturn a law passed in 1970, which permitted divorce under certain conditions. Italian women felt differently – without a divorce law they could be tied for life to an absent or cruel husband. When the Italian government held a **referendum** in 1974, women voted massively in favour of divorce. Later, women also clashed with the Church on access to **contraception** and **abortion**.

Having it all?

On the surface, many things appeared to have changed for the better, especially in Western countries. Girls did as well and often better than boys in schools and colleges. More women studied in further education and successfully competed for jobs with men. On average, women married later, had children later, and many more combined children and a career. There was more openness about sex, and more acceptance of single women, including **lesbians**. There were more women leaders in every field, including business and politics. There were claims that women really could 'have it all' – beauty, career, money, home, motherhood. Attitudes and barriers that had previously restrained women crumbled or were ignored.

However, society still seemed to be divided along gender lines. There were still 'male' jobs and 'female' jobs, with male jobs inevitably paying more. For example, in the UK, thirty years after the Equal Pay Act of 1970

Women against violence

Many feminists have campaigned against war and violence, in personal protests and mass demonstrations. Some of the most active campaigns were against the development of nuclear weapons. Feminists also took their concerns to the **United Nations**. At the 1993 World Conference on **Human Rights**, women directed many of the meetings, including a Global Tribunal on Violations of Women's Human Rights, which heard personal accounts from women from many countries. One participant said: 'We came there and took the place by storm. We took over. And they [the UN] realized very quickly that the energy and ideas and organizing were coming from the women.'

Many more women have risen to management positions, but most still get paid less than a man in a similar job.

most of the workers in the low-wage 'female' occupations of catering, cleaning and caring, and 70 per cent of those receiving the minimum wage, were women. Rather than 'having it all', women were constantly juggling the different facets of their lives – paid work, housework, childcare. More women were bringing up children without a partner, on low incomes or inadequate **social security**.

Yet most women did not see themselves as feminists. In part, this was because of the distorted image of feminism displayed in the media. Like the **suffragettes**, feminists were depicted as ugly, aggressive, humourless man-haters, often as lesbians. Feminism seemed the opposite of femininity. Most women wanted to look and feel good and enjoy life, to attract men, find a partner and have children. Feminism didn't seem to say very much about

Many women bring up their families alone, on low incomes and in inadequate housing.

In her book of 2001, *Kiss my Tiara: How to Rule the World as a Smartmouth Goddess*, the author Susan Jane Gilman says:

'For women today, feminism is often perceived as dreary.... And to some extent it's true. I'm not knocking the women's movement of past years. I'm a huge advocate and beneficiary of choice, workplace legislation and domestic violence legislation.... But the problem is that a lot of feminist ideology simply doesn't translate well into real life. It doesn't empower women on a practical level.'

these goals. At the same time, most women did believe that they should be treated equally with men in the wider world, to earn their own money and make their own choices. So it wasn't surprising that, when faced with inequalities or injustices, many women would say: 'I'm not a feminist, but... '

Entering the mainstream

By the 1990s, although many formerly **radical** feminist ideas had entered mainstream life most feminist writing and research took place within universities. Many universities had established courses and departments in women's studies and had appointed professors, lecturers and researchers producing a stream of journals, studies and books, by and about women. They seemed to spend more time writing about feminism than finding practical ways to improve women's lives. Yet sometimes arguments spilled over into the outside world.

Feminists protest that beauty contests present women as 'sex objects'.

Exploitation

One of the most fervent areas of discussion concerned sex and the way women's bodies were viewed and used. From the 1970s onwards, there was more openness about sexual matters, including sex before marriage, divorce and lesbianism, and greater freedom to produce and display **pornography**. Women's Liberation had urged women to look, dress and behave to suit themselves rather than as 'sex objects' to please men. It had protested against beauty contests, sexist advertisements and pornography, saying that they degraded and exploited women.

Women and their bodies

In 2002, French feminists were divided over a call by a woman Member of Parliament (MP) to introduce legal brothels. The woman MP argued that it would protect sex workers and improve their conditions of work. Gisele Halimi, a leading feminist, opposed her saying: *'No woman chooses freely to make her body the object of exchange of money for pleasure.'* Elizabeth Badinter, another feminist, stated: *'If a woman prefers to earn in two nights what she couldn't earn in a month working in a factory, who can decide in her place how she should use her body?'*

Indian sex workers protest against discrimination and ask for rights in Calcutta, March 2002.

From the 1980s, the issue of pornography and the sex industry came to the fore. Some feminists argued that pornography was a hugely dangerous and exploitative industry, which profited from degrading women who were forced or tricked into doing such work. These feminists wanted pornography banned and sex-shops closed. Women held 'reclaim the night' marches through 'red light' areas of strip clubs and brothels. Other feminists had different views. They argued that pornography was a symptom, not a cause, of women's oppression. Some thought that some types of pornography could be liberating for women. Others did not approve of pornography, but felt that banning it would not be helpful. They argued instead for legal regulation of pornography. However, all feminists condemned the growing involvement of children and young girls and the violence and criminal activity that existed in much of the sex industry.

While mass feminist actions seemed to be waning in Western countries, feminist activity emerged in Latin America, Asia, Africa and the Middle

THE HENLEY COLLEGE LIBRARY

East. While the overall aims remained the same – to promote the rights of women – feminism reflected the very different situations faced by women there.

In Latin America, women struggled against 'machismo' – the idea that men must be dominant over women at home, work and leisure – and the Roman Catholic Church, which opposes divorce, contraception and abortion. Yet it was often women who kept families together, either as single parents or as main earners. Many feminists were active in left-wing political movements and were jailed, killed or 'disappeared' during military dictatorships. In Argentina, a remarkable group of women, known as the Mothers of the Plaza de Mayo, met each week in the main

The women known as the Mothers of the Plaza de Mayo have spent years in silent protest in support of human rights in Argentina.

square of Buenos Aires. There they staged silent protests against the 'disappearances' of their children and other human rights abuses by the Argentine government. Despite threats, they have continued their vigil for years, gaining worldwide recognition and respect.

Women workers in Southeast Asia, like these young women in Cambodia, work long hours for little pay.

Sweat shops

In the rapidly industrializing countries of Southeast Asia, feminists focused on the situation of young women working in giant factories, making garments and assembling electronic goods. Although wages were higher than in farming or domestic work, hours were long and conditions oppressive. **Trade unions** were not recognized and strikes were forbidden. Far worse was the situation of thousands of girls and young women working in the bars and brothels of big cities like Bangkok, Manila and Phnom Penh. Some lived in conditions amounting to slavery.

Andrea Dworkin (1946-)

Andrea Dworkin is an American feminist campaigner and author who has carried out research into the relationship between male violence and women's inequality. Her controversial work focuses on pornography which, she argues, violates the human rights of all women. She helped to draft anti-pornography laws that have now been applied in some US cities.

Women in India

One of the most widespread and **militant** feminist movements developed in India where traditional prejudices remained active in the face of change. Some middle-class women had been inspired by Women's Liberation, but even more important were their encounters with the poverty and oppression in India itself. While a woman did not inherit family land or property, she could be ill-treated and abandoned by her husband's family. Girls received less schooling than boys, and huge numbers of women remained unable to read or write. In most homes, women were expected to prepare and serve food and eat last and least after their husbands, brothers and sons.

Child marriage is still practised in some parts of India.

Inequality in India

The Progressive Organization of Women (POW) was one of India's earliest feminist groups. Its 1974 manifesto proclaimed:

*'The concept of the Indian woman as an equal partner of man... has never been so closely shattered as it is today. We have, on the one hand, our constitution mouthing pious platitudes about the equality of women... and on the other, the terrible conditions of the majority of Indian women.... Eighty-seven out of every hundred women cannot read or write. The horrible practices of prostitution, child marriage, **purdah** and **dowry** have cut at the very root of the dignity of women.'*

Many women in Bangladesh have left their villages for factory jobs in the cities. Now they are demanding equal rights with men.

Greater prosperity had created its own forms of discrimination. A woman normally brought a dowry of money or property to her new husband's household. But some husbands began to demand higher dowries and to abuse or even kill women who could not meet their demands. Women's organizations sprang up across the vast country to campaign against injustices including unfair laws, domestic violence, dowry deaths and pre-birth sex testing (to determine whether the baby would be a wished-for boy rather than a girl). But there were also more positive campaigns to teach women their rights, for better education and healthcare, and greater economic opportunities.

The women's court

For fifteen years the people of 350 villages in central India have been taking their domestic disputes to an informal court where the judges are four middle-aged women. The court started after the Women's Welfare Centre, a feminist organization, began teaching village women about their rights, but it now operates independently. The judges deal with cases of marriage breakups, domestic violence and land disputes; they also explain about people's rights. Local people and the police prefer the women's court to the law courts because they trust the judges to act fairly and know that they never delay a hearing or a verdict.

Women against apartheid

In South Africa feminism was directly related to the long political struggle against the **apartheid** system, where the country was ruled upon racial lines, with black women facing the greatest discrimination. Women's organizations played an important part in the fight against apartheid. With the end of apartheid and the introduction of **democracy** during the 1990s, women gained full democratic rights alongside men. But while some women have done well, most women continue to live in bad housing, bringing up children on low, irregular incomes. Women and girls are especially affected by HIV/AIDS and suffer extreme levels of violence and sexual abuse.

In most African and Middle Eastern countries, feminist movements are still new and have yet to make much impact. Where they exist, feminist organizations focus on challenging customs and traditional laws that support male dominance, such as polygamy (where a man can be married to several women at the same time), unfair divorces, discrimination against widows (who lose their home, land and **status** after the death of their husbands) and **female genital mutilation**. But the biggest problem is widespread and growing poverty often coupled with bad and corrupt government, civil war and ethnic or religious conflict, and the terrible toil of disease, especially HIV/AIDS. All of these factors pose huge challenges for feminism in the years ahead.

Women on the move: Palestinian women take part in the World March for Women in Lebanon, September 2002.

Beijing and Beyond

For most of its history feminism has been a **radical** minority movement. Feminists have been ignored, shunned, scorned, ridiculed – even imprisoned and killed – for their ideas and actions. Despite this, feminists have always been ambitious, believing that they will eventually triumph.

Many feminist ideas that were once considered impossible are now **human rights** standards. In 1975, the **United Nations** launched a UN Decade for Women with a conference in Mexico City attended by 133 governments and 6,000 women from **non-government organizations** (NGOs). Twenty years later, the third Women's Conference in Beijing was attended by 189 governments and 30,000 feminists from NGOs worldwide. Increasingly it was these feminists who were making governments and international institutions act on women's issues.

Women join together at a ceremony at the UN Women's Conference in Beijing, China in 1995.

★ International rights

When the United Nations first declared that it would develop international standards for women's rights many feminists were uninterested or sceptical. They saw the UN as a distant organization, dominated by men. But between 1975 and 1985 feminists became more involved, especially when the new Convention on the Elimination of All Forms of Discrimination Against Women (CEDAW) came into force in 1981. Almost every country has signed CEDAW with one notable exception – the USA.

Women from Iran at the 1995 Women's Conference in Beijing hold banners proclaiming that Islam supports women's rights.

Empowerment

Research by United Nations agencies revealed that 70 per cent of the world's poorest people are women and girls. Faced with this huge challenge, many feminists have changed their focus from gaining individual and legal equality or promoting radical changes to finding practical ways to help women overcome the barriers of poverty and custom. This is often described as '**empowerment**' – enabling women to have enough power to make changes for themselves. Empowerment takes many forms, including **literacy** and **numeracy** projects, small-scale savings and loans schemes, and advice on **contraception** and protection against HIV/AIDS.

Measuring women's worth

During the Decade for Women the UN tried to determine women's situation worldwide. In 1980 it reported:

'Although women are 50 per cent of the world adult population, they comprise one third of the labour force, perform nearly two thirds of hours, receive only one tenth of world inc own less than 1 per cent of world proper

Women on the board

In Norway, women have equal rights in law, education and work and 40 per cent of the seats in Parliament. However, only 7.3 per cent of company directors are women. The Norwegian government plans to pass a law that will increase the number of women on company boards to 40 per cent by 2005. Laila Daavoey, a government minister, said that the law would help companies by promoting greater diversity and experience and that most opposition came from men who were unwilling to give up their powerful positions.

Women in Afghanistan covered by the traditional burka. The Taleban government (1995-2001) punished women who did not wear this garment.

Although there are huge gaps between women in rich and poor countries, they also have things in common. More women are in paid work, or want to be in paid work, than ever before. This is partly because it is necessary for many women to bring in a wage to support their families. There are more single, separated and divorced women bringing up children without support from partners or their extended family than ever before. More women now use modern contraceptives, causing birth rates to fall worldwide. And in most countries, more girls attend school and college and go on to earn more and live longer than their mothers.

An ongoing struggle

However, women's rights can move backwards as well as forwards. In Russia, after the communist system ended in 1991, women began to lose rights they had once taken for granted. As the Russian economy collapsed, the government declared that men should have priority in jobs, even though women were better educated and many were supporting families on their own. Russian women showed little interest in feminist ideas as they struggled to survive in the harsh economic climate. In Afghanistan, the situation was much worse. There, women lost the few rights they possessed after the country came under the rule of the Taleban (1995–2001). The Taleban regime claimed to follow the only true form of Islam. While the Qur'an supported rights for women, the Taleban banned women from most paid work and kept girls from school. Women regarded as disobedient were punished with public beatings. The Taleban has now gone, but Afghan women still face enormous hardships.

The future

In Western countries, there are many views about the future of feminism. Some people say that we belong to a post-feminist era, where women have achieved equality with men and therefore no longer need feminism. Others fear that many feminist gains will be lost – one influential American book was even called *Backlash* and described the reaction against the women's rights movement. Still others talk about a new feminist movement of younger women – sometimes called 'third-wave feminism' – based upon empowerment and personal freedom in dress, manner, speech and music, and support for radical causes, such as the environment, animal rights, **lesbian** and gay rights. And there are still many women, probably the majority, who just want to see women treated fairly and equally, with respect and dignity, as they get on with their daily lives.

Young women at the UN Women's Conference in 1995. The future of feminism is in their hands.

Date List

1404	Christine of Pizan writes 'The City of Ladies'.
1776	American Revolution and the Declaration of Independence.
1789	French Revolution and the Declaration of the Rights of Man.
1791	Olympe de Gouges writes *A Declaration of the Rights of Woman*.
1792	Mary Wollstonecraft writes *A Vindication of the Rights of Women*.
1848	First American Women's Rights Convention at Seneca Falls accepts the Declaration of Sentiments, based on the Declaration of Independence.
1867	John Stuart Mill, British MP, presents petition for women's suffrage to the House of Commons.
1869	Elizabeth Cady Stanton and Susan B. Anthony establish the National Women's Suffrage Association in New York.
1878	US Congress is presented with, and rejects, a constitutional amendment for women's suffrage.
1893	Women gain the vote in New Zealand.
1895	First known use of the term 'feminist'.
1902	Women gain the vote in Australia.
1903	Emmeline and Christabel Pankhurst form the Women's Social and Political Union (WSPU).
1905	Women gain the vote in Finland.
1913-17	Women gain the vote in Norway (1913), Denmark and Iceland (1915), Canada (1917).
1918-19	Women gain the vote in Austria, Estonia, Germany, Ireland, Latvia, Poland, UK (women over 30), USSR (following Russian Revolution of 1917) (all 1918); Belgium, Luxembourg, Netherlands, Sweden (all 1919).
1920	Women gain the vote in Albania, Czechoslovakia, USA (Nineteenth Amendment to the Constitution).
1928	Women gain the vote at the age of twenty-one in the UK.
1944	Women gain the vote in France.
1949	Simone de Beauvoir's book *The Second Sex* is published in France; an English translation follows in 1953.
1963	Betty Friedan's book *The Feminine Mystique* is published in the USA.
1966	National Union of Women (NOW) formed in the USA.
1966–80	Era of Women's Liberation with groups, activities, books etc. in North America, Western Europe, Australia and elsewhere.
1970	UK government passes Equal Pay Act.
1972	US Congress passes Equal Rights Amendment (ERA) for states to ratify (lapses in 1982 after failure to ratify).
1974	Women in Italy vote massively in favour of legalization of divorce.
1975	Women in Iceland hold first ever women's strike.
1975	UN Conference in Mexico City launches UN Decade for Women.
1979	UN adopts Convention on the Elimination of All Forms of Discrimination Against Women; it comes into force in 1981.
1985	Second UN Conference for Women in Nairobi, Kenya.
1994	Black women gain the vote and participate in the first democratic, multiracial elections in South Africa.
1995	Third UN Conference for Women in Beijing, China. The UN also adopts the Gender-Related Development Index, which attempts to measure women's economic, social and political wellbeing in every UN member country.
1998	The International Court declares that rape is a war crime when used by the military and as torture when practised in prisons.

Glossary

abortion
ending a pregnancy in the first months following conception.

activist
a person who takes direct and often militant action to achieve an end.

allied countries
those countries (USA, UK, Australia etc.) that fought against the Axis powers (Germany, Italy, Japan) in the Second World War (1939-45).

amendment
alteration at a later date to an existing document.

anti-feminist
a person who opposes feminism.

apartheid
meaning 'apartness', the political system applied in South Africa (1948-94) in which white people had full political and economic rights and black people had few rights.

capitalist system
an economic system based upon private ownership of business and trade.

censorship
the banning or changing of books, films, letters etc. that are felt to be obscene or politically unacceptable.

Chartist
a British political movement between 1838 and 1848, which called for reform of Parliament and male suffrage.

civil rights movement
a non-violent political movement to establish black equality in the USA, lead by Martin Luther King Jr.

communism
a political theory based on state ownership of industry, where each person is paid and works according to their needs. A communist is a supporter of communism.

constitution
a document that sets out a country's principles and standards.

contraception
the prevention of pregnancy by using contraceptives (e.g. condoms, the pill etc.).

convention
a meeting or a legal agreement.

democracy
a political system based on equality under the law, an elected government and fair and regular elections.

despotic
ruling alone without consultation.

direct action
coordinated activities e.g. demonstrations, marches etc.

dowry
money or property a woman receives on marriage.

empowerment
enabling women to tackle their own problems, such as poverty, unfair laws and customs, low status etc., through sharing ideas and practical actions.

fascism
a political system based on extreme patriotism, racial and sexual inequality, a strong leader and government and military strength.

female genital mutilation
a traditional practice in parts of Africa in which all or part of a woman's external sex organs are removed. The procedure is usually carried out in childhood.

gender roles
the roles females and males play in society and how society expects them to behave. While gender roles are related to our biological sex (female or male) they are determined by society, not biology.

guardianship
legal responsibility for someone.

human rights
basic rights that belong to every human being.

labour movement
a movement of working-class people to improve their living and employment conditions.

law reform
improving laws or the justice system.

lesbian
a woman who is sexually attracted to women.

liberal
belief in freedom of thought, speech, action and religion, and tolerance towards others.

literacy
being able to read and write.

militant
extremely active in support of a cause.

non-government organization (NGO)
a group or organization which aims to help people or provide a service without making a profit. Sometimes called a charity.

numeracy
being able to use numbers, particularly in arithmetic.

oral contraceptives
pills taken by mouth to prevent pregnancy.

pacifist
someone who believes in the peaceful resolution of conflicts.

philosopher
a person who studies the rightness of beliefs, thoughts and actions.

philosophy
system of ideas or beliefs.

pornography
words or images describing sexual acts in detail.

purdah
a practice in which women are kept secluded from outsiders.

radical
favouring ideas or actions different from the mainstream.

referendum
a single vote on an important issue.

revolution
overthrowing the existing political system.

sexual equality
when women and men have equal rights and responsibilities in law and practice.

socialism
a political movement based upon government action and public ownership. An original aim of socialism was to support workers rather than private enterprise.

socialist parties
political parties originally based in the working class that support greater equality by working for gradual change through Parliament.

social security
benefits paid by the government, e.g.

unemployment, maternity, housing or illness benefit.

status
rank or place in society.

subversive
undermining the established order.

suffrage
the right to vote.

suffragette
a suffragist who supported direct action.

suffragist
a person who supports votes for women.

trade union
an organization of workers campaigning for better wages and conditions.

United Nations
an international body, formed in 1945, with almost all the world's countries as members. It sets international standards, aims to resolve conflicts and manages relief and development programmes.

vindication
arguments in support of a cause.

Women's Liberation
a mass feminist movement, mainly in North America and Europe but also other countries, between 1965 and 1980.

Resources

There are thousands of books about feminist ideas and women's studies. Most are academic studies; there are few resources for teachers or younger people.

Background reading and reference
A Century of Women – The History of Women in Britain and the United States, Sheila Rowbotham, Penguin, 1999

Human Development Report 2004, United Nations Development Programme, 2004

People's Century edited by Godfrey Hodgson, BBC Books, 1995-6, two volumes

The Atlas of Women, Joni Seager, Oxfam, 2003

Information for younger people
100 Greatest Women, Michael Pollard, Belitha, 1995

Justice at the Door! The Struggle for Women's Equality (1830-1930), Jean Holder and Katherine Milcoy, Fawcett Library, 1997-8

Emmeline Pankhurst, Margaret Hudson, Heinemann Library, 1998

Feminism for Teenagers, Sophie Grillet, Piccadilly Press, 1997

The Changing Role of Women, Mandy Ross, 20th Century Perspectives series, Heinemann Library, 2003

The Other Half of History series, Fiona Macdonald, Belitha Press, 2000. Includes *Women in Peace and War (1900-1945)* and *Women in a Changing World (1945-2000)*

The Suffragettes in Pictures, Diana Atkinson, Sutton Publishing, 1996

Index